children and bereavement

Wendy Duffy

2nd edition

To my husband Peter and the family

Church House Publishing
Church House
Great Smith Street
London SW1P 3NZ

ISBN 0 7151 4998 9

First edition published in 1995 by The
National Society and Church House Publishing
Second edition published 2003 by Church
House Publishing

Cover design by Church House Publishing
Printed by Creative Print and Design Group,
Ebbw Vale, Wales

Contents

Acknowledgements

Extracts from the *New Revised Standard Version of the Bible* © 1989 by the Division of Christian Education of the National Council of Churches of Christ in the USA. Used by permission. All rights reserved.

Extracts from *Common Worship: Pastoral Services*, Church House Publishing, 2000 and *The Prayer Book as Proposed in 1928* are copyright © The Archbishops' Council and reproduced by permission.

Penguin Books: an extract from *Watership Down* by Richard Adams.

National Society/Church House Publishing for prayers from *Prayers for Children* by Christopher Herbert.

Christopher Herbert: 'And when it comes to our feelings' from *Words of Comfort*, second edition, Church House Publishing, 2000.

Marjorie Pizer, Cremorne, Australia: 'The existence of love' from *Poems for Comfort and Healing*, Pizer, Bookmart Ltd, 1992, originally entitled 'To you the living'.

Darton, Longman & Todd: extracts from *Prayers from a Troubled Heart* by George Appleton.

Foreword

The topic of children and bereavement is one that has been neglected for far too long. This second edition of Wendy Duffy's book is a very welcome step in addressing some of the difficult questions which this subject raises.

This book is an outstanding combination of practical advice and thoughtful reflection on all areas of this important subject. It draws on a wealth of real experience, offers thought-provoking insights into the world of a bereaved child and explores some of the similarities and differences between bereaved adults and children. It also offers a wealth of resources, including a selection of prayers and readings which might be used at funerals or services of memorial, addresses of organizations where people may find help, and a selection of books suitable for use with different age groups.

Children and Bereavement should be considered required reading for anyone who is likely to come into contact with children who have experienced death and loss: clergy and readers, funeral directors, teachers, doctors and nurses. It would also be useful for non-professionals who simply want to find out more, for example the friends and family of a bereaved child.

If our society were to consider some of Wendy Duffy's suggestions, it is possible that many bereaved children might make the transition into adulthood with fewer difficulties and without bearing the emotional scars of their bereavement for the rest of their lives.

I warmly commend this excellent book.

Revd Tim Alban-Jones MBE

Vicar of Soham and Wicken

And when it comes to our feelings, those who have been left behind discover a vast ocean. Sometimes the ocean seems calm and still, and yet the next minute, for no apparent reason, a wave comes crashing over us. At other times the loss is so intense it is like being at sea, out of the sight of land and simply tossed around; and then, sometimes there are moments of quiet and serene beauty as a new truth dawns, and sometimes the grief is so overwhelming that it's like drowning, and there's no one to hear our cries.

The Rt Revd Christopher Herbert

Bishop of St Albans

1 'I don't know what to say...'

Working in a hospice and parish alongside patients and their families has been a tremendous privilege for me over the years. It has provided an opportunity to learn about death and dying, and it has shown that dying is unique and personal to everyone. How we cope with our 'big dying' may well depend on how we have coped with and been supported through all our little dyings.

Every year thousands of children face bereavement, perhaps through the death of a grandparent, parent, friend or sibling, but, because adults are often so deeply engrossed in their own grief, the feelings of the children involved may not even be noticed. Professional helpers often see them as 'resilient' or 'brave', or they are assumed to be unable to understand what is going on. It is the passionate theme of this book that children matter and that their processes of bereavement and grieving ought to be taken seriously.

How we help children during their losses can have a profound effect on the way their own lives will develop in the future, and even the way in which they will face their own death. The task facing those of us who help children through death and bereavement is not easy but it may be a privilege, for children often bring to the process a freshness and wisdom (and sometimes a sense of the divine) which can be deeply moving.

Often our first reaction will be to think, 'I don't know what to say...'. Rather than having a go and getting it wrong, we say nothing and leave it to somebody else; so another child lives through another missed opportunity and thinks we don't care about them. The truth is that sometimes we care more about our own feelings; in sparing them we are protecting ourselves. It must be a mistake to do nothing in case we fail. Perhaps it would be better to try and do what we can in spite of our feelings of inadequacy and build bridges instead of walls. It can be lonely behind walls.

Our television screens bombard us with death. We see so much of it that we have almost become immune to it. Always someone else is dealing with it: the United Nations, the Red Cross, the armed forces, rescue services, specialists, experts. We can send donations and there our responsibility ends. All we have to do then is change the programme, confident that we've done our bit.

At some point, however, the buck will stop and it will be up to you. Just for a moment that child needs you. Hopefully it won't be as dramatic as that. If, however, you do find yourself on the spot, don't despair. It's amazing how often we seem to be given the words and actions appropriate to the occasion – sometimes with such presence of mind and with such confidence that in retrospect and with hindsight we later wonder what on earth came over us. I remember experiencing this with Jamie, the pale, pinched seven-year-old son of Linda and John.

John had died just over a year before in the hospice. Linda and Jamie's teachers were worried that Jamie hadn't begun to settle, one of the reasons being that he was convinced his Daddy was still in the bed where he had died – where Jamie had last seen him. We talked it over with Linda, with the hospice social worker, and with the staff who had got to know the family quite closely, and it was decided that I should be the one to 'put Jamie right'.The buck had stopped. Between us, the nurses and I drew butterflies, falling leaves and flowers. We wrote cute stories in coloured felt tips, included some prayers, and went to great lengths to 'get it right' for Jamie and his Mum. I still didn't know what I was going to say – not really. If I prayed it would have been, 'Thy will be done'. We met at the door of the ward – the social worker, Jamie, his Mum and me. The nurses had vanished. The moment had come and there he was, still pale and pinched, a little taller, and more bouncy than I had expected. He walked straight past me to John's bed. 'That's my Daddy's bed,' he said.

That was my cue. I picked Jamie up and sat down on the bed with him on my knee and we went from there. We reminisced about his Daddy, about all the things they had done together, and remembered the things that Jamie could now do well because he'd been taught by his Daddy. There was something about football, he could tell the time, and he'd still got his Daddy's watch . . . We ended up reading part of the epilogue of *Watership Down* (quoted in the readings at the end of this book), by which time I was in a heap. Moved by the sensitivity that children have, we hugged each other and agreed that Daddy was all right now – whatever that means. And it did seem all right for then. He came back once or twice and revisited his Daddy's bed, but it did indeed seem all right. On the day after he'd gone I wondered how he would be, if I'd said too much, or not enough – and that's the way of it, isn't it?

Whether someone has just died or whether someone else is ill and there is the painful possibility that they will soon die it somehow helps to prepare. Forewarned is forearmed. To have time to think about where we are at – each one of us – before we start talking to our children about the death of someone close, or death in general, we need to try to understand the whys and the wherefores and the weariness and the multiplicity of feelings that make up bereavement.

It is important to understand that for each one of us it has been or will be different . . . that you and I and our friends and neighbours will bring to it our own agendas, our own beliefs, our own hopes, our own guilt and anger, and in our own time our acceptance and recovery and growth.

We should look back into our own childhood to remember how bereavement felt and use or improve on that. Sadness and grief make children of us all, and we learn that it is something to be worked through and carried around, not left behind or got over. From time to time we will want to revisit it, like Jamie, but having learned that that too is all right, we will have treasure to hand on to our own children – our gift to them, part of their inheritance.

Understanding separation and loss in our own adult lives

We may well feel bewildered and even helpless when thinking about caring for a bereaved child, and that is understandable. But if we are first prepared to think through our own understanding of bereavement and loss, this will give us real insights on how to help children. Most of us, at some time in our lives, will be faced with the death of someone we care deeply about. We need to look at our understanding of ourselves, our personal experience of grief, our reactions to it and how we cope.

Mourning is not a sign of weakness; it is a necessity for the good of our health and general well-being. Although each of us reacts to loss in different ways, and at different times, there are recognized stages which affect us. We go through these various stages (and revisit them) in the mourning process and for each person the process is unique. What follows is only a rough guide to the stages of bereavement. It is descriptive not prescriptive.

Shock/numbness

The feeling of shock on hearing that someone close has died has been described as a huge blow, akin to physical trauma. The senses reel, the legs tremble and the stomach churns. It is no wonder that some people faint, or at least need to find a chair to sit down. Others become unusually calm and detached, others become confused and unable to take in what has happened – hearing the words yet unable to believe what they are hearing – until later, sometimes hours or days later.

Denial and disbelief: searching and yearning

> 'It can't be…It can't be…'

> 'I felt him sit down on the bed beside me and I knew he'd come back.'

> 'I just can't believe it…'

For a while it seems impossible to believe that someone who was alive so recently is now no longer.

> 'I hear the car on the gravel; his voice in the supermarket; the key in the lock.'

> 'The phone rings and I think – that'll be him.'

The bereaved begin to think that they are going out of their mind; they can't believe that normal rational people can do such 'silly' things. They need constant reassurance that it is part of a normal process.

People complain that they can't remember things – even simple things including the normal everyday routine. They pick things up and put them down again, feeling listless and uninterested, unable to concentrate and with little or no purpose in life. They often say, 'What's the point, I've nothing to live for any more…'. Despite feeling tired – emotion and sadness are very draining – a good night's sleep seems to be impossible. They lie awake for what seems like hours, going over it all, replaying the video of the events leading up to the death, but gradually it begins to settle.

So the bereaved continue to exist while all these feelings wash over and around them; no sooner reaching a point of 'feeling better' when another wave of questioning, reasoning and revisiting appears as if from nowhere.

But in between there are glimpses of hope and light and the realization that although life will never be the same again, it will and does go on, if differently. The investment in the past can eventually be seen as a treasure house of joy – a gift that might otherwise never have been. Our memories cannot be taken from us, though they may fade, hence the importance of family gatherings and 'Do you remember when…?'. Although these hurts and disappointments also fade, they too are memories and make us what we are.

Slowly, slowly we discover that we are tackling things that need to be done that we'd never done before and had always thought to be impossible – cooking, household repairs, accounts, blocked drains. At first we may need help from someone to show us what to do, but as our dependency lessens and we grow in confidence and become more independent, we find we can cope.

Little deaths

We tend to think of bereavement as grieving only when someone we love has died, but many life situations can and do have a similar effect on us. These might include:

The shock of redundancy and unemployment;

The wrench of moving house and leaving friends behind and having to start again;

Close friends or family moving away or going abroad to live and work;

The breakdown of a relationship resulting in separation or divorce;

The necessity of a hysterectomy in the case of a young couple longing to have children;

The discovery that someone we love has a serious illness;

Children leaving home;

Failure to achieve;

Burglary.

Just how we cope with a particular crisis depends on what our personality allows, but it also depends on our environment, family, upbringing and example, and someone we trust to help us carry the load. Whether out of fear or panic or guilt or self-pity, it helps to share it with an understanding listener – a minister or a wise and trusted friend. To allow ourselves to cry, to shout in anger and to laugh too, helps us to experience the pain and come through it.

Grief and mourning are a journey and it is only by taking part in the journey that real understanding comes.

It is by recognizing these processes in ourselves as adults that we can begin to empathize deeply with the bereaved – and it is from the deep spiritual well of our own experience that we will draw healing and refreshment and be able to offer support, wisdom and love to a bereaved child.

2 Children's perceptions of death

In 1943 Claire Mulholland published a book of poems written to and about her daughter who had died of leukaemia. The shortest said simply:

> Worst of all was the agony
> of not knowing
> what you knew…

It is safer to assume that young children do understand (at their levels and in their ways) more than we give them credit for. How and what they understand at a particular age and stage is of course important but, as with all generalizations, not to be taken as prescriptive for the particular individual with whom you are dealing. Rosemary Wells writes:

> 'Up to adolescence and beyond, all children are more afraid of the separation from loved people than of the death itself, even their own death. And what happens afterwards is nearly always "heaven".'

Infant/toddler

A baby or very young child has no understanding that a parent has 'died', but will sense their absence and feel the sadness in the atmosphere at home. According to Elisabeth Kubler-Ross: 'Up to the age of three a child is concerned only about separation'.

Separation anxiety may to some extent be avoided if a familiar adult or parent is able to provide continuity and 'normality' while the family reorganizes.

A baby may react by showing irritability, erratic eating, sleeping and crying patterns, or tummy upsets. Temporary emotional withdrawal is a possibility until security and stability can be re-established.

Three to five years

Psychologist Maria Nagy writes:

> 'In these early years the permanence of death is not yet realised – it is seen as a vague concept, something that happens to flowers, insects and pets. Children tend to see death as akin to sleep or a journey, from which one can wake up or return. Questions are asked and children seem to require no more information than they ask at one time.'

John, aged five, dug up the goldfish each day, for several days, 'just to see how he was getting on'. In his own way he was trying to understand what this 'dying' was all about.

Other people, however, feel that children, even at such a young age, are deeply aware of the permanence of death in terms of a life beyond this present one.

> 'My rabbit died. He went to rabbit heaven. Heaven is in the sky where Jesus is.'

When this quotation was overheard (in reception class), the child looked up to the top of a classroom cupboard – and most of the children followed her look. There were no more comments from them.

The children were then able to express very vividly what their own sadness felt like. Rebecca, aged five, had a kitten which had been killed. She explained that she 'felt sadness in her middle' and the pointed to her ribs just above her tummy. They were also able to have a go at defining what they meant by heaven: 'Heaven is love,' said Janice, 'and it goes on for ever . . .'. Naturally they find the whole concept difficult to express. Amanda, aged five, said, 'I don't want to go to heaven. It's underground up in the sky'.

Seven to nine years

It is during this period that children generally develop the concept of the permanence of death, understanding that death means no longer being able to eat, sleep, laugh, cry or feel pain. Possible signs of fear need reassurance and comfort.

> Anna, aged eight, told us that Grandpa had died and gone to heaven.
>
> 'Where's heaven, Anna?'
>
> 'A place of peace,' was the reply.

Death is familiarized by TV as something that happens on the news and films, but never as close as home. Kelly writes:

> 'Death means to me the loss of a friend. It's not moving away to send postcards and letters, but forever.'

Alice writes:

> 'When someone dies it brings unhappiness and grief, misery and sorrow. Death means to me that they have gone forever and I will only see them when I go to heaven.'

Nine to twelve years

At this age children can be very 'matter of fact', and their acceptance of death as a fact of life is no exception.

> 'What is death, Giles?' (aged eleven)
>
> 'Loss of life, of course,' came the reply.
>
> 'We were sorry to hear that your Grandma had died.'
>
> 'Oh, that's OK. She was old, you know.'

Rebecca writes:

> 'You die, and you leave the world. Your body is no longer living and you rot away. Your ashes turn into earth and the wind blows your body away in the world.'

Twelve years through adolescence

Adolescence is the time when children are searching for identity, searching for meaning and asking 'Why?'. Death at this stage can be a profound experience and in order to cope they may regress to earlier concepts and then work through to more adult understanding. Meanwhile, mood swings, refusal to cooperate at home and 'bad behaviour' at school require a deal of patience and understanding.

In her powerful book *Your Friend Rebecca*, Linda Hoy describes the pain and turmoil experienced by Rebecca after her mother has died, as she tries to cope with her grossly insensitive schoolteacher 'The Hog'.

> 'That's all there is in their lives, Rebecca: cooking and knitting.' She snarls these words at me as if they're the most obscene expressions in the English language. 'Knitting and cooking and washing-up.'
>
> I see the jars of blackberry jam, piled up high and labelled in the pantry. Each with its neat little label edged in blue. I see her face again as she stands by the cooker…the sobs start heaving their way up inside my throat. I swallow hard and try to force them back, but this great mound of sadness is struggling to erupt and it's unbearable…
>
> Before I even know what's happening, I find myself standing up and facing her. My cheeks are burning red with hatred and my fists are clenched as tight as rocks…
>
> 'I hate you!' I shout at her. And then I take a deep breath and scream out in a voice they must be able to hear right out in the playground, 'Just bloody well leave me alone!'

3 Stages of grief

Early grief

Shock

On hearing the news that someone you love has died, your first reaction is often numbness, or sometimes acute panic followed by numbness. There may be a sense of watching the event as if it were happening to someone else. This lack of sensation may last from a few hours to a week. It alternates with outbursts of extremely intense distress or anger or both, as the reality of the loss begins to register, leading to intense pining, heightened irritability and sobbing or crying out loud for the lost person. If it falls to you to have to break the news, it is best to be there, face to face, to hold and support, and to stay alongside for a while. There is only one way to tell the truth and that is clearly, slowly and gently, not being afraid to use the words *death* and *dying.*

Crying may not come at first – more of a stunned, silent bewilderment, but when it comes be thankful. We need to cry to release feelings of despair, hurt, anger and the rest – the overwhelming feelings of sorrow and loneliness that threaten to engulf like a tidal wave. No one is exempt from feelings though we express them in different ways and some with great difficulty. We need to reassure the bereaved that it is perfectly normal 'allowed' behaviour to cry and to be in a state of shock, and that they should not be ashamed of it, or of crying in front of others and indeed with the children.

A very young child may feel a sense of painful confusion because he or she is quite unable to understand the general state of upset within the family and the home.

Numbness

C. S. Lewis in his book *A Grief Observed*, written after his wife died, said this:

> 'No one ever told me that grief felt so like fear. I am not afraid, but the sensation is like being afraid. The same fluttering in the stomach, the same restlessness, the yawning. I keep swallowing. At other times it feels like being mildly drunk or concussed. There is a sort of invisible blanket between the world and me. I find it hard to take in what anyone says.'

'It was all happening around me but I wasn't part of it' describes the state of numbness, as if a heavy blow has deadened all feeling. This seems to be nature's way of easing the pain. We can only take in so much at a time; this way information is filtered and we do as we must for life to continue from day to day.

It is in the days immediately following the death of a loved one, when the bereaved are struggling with the reality of the situation, that decisions have to be made – the painful process of telling other people what has happened, again and again, the registration of the death, discussions with the undertaker to arrange the funeral, a visit from the minister to discuss an Order of Service, the choice of hymns, readings and music. Some people throw themselves into a frenzy of activity, grateful to have plenty to do, and can see the funeral and the gathering afterwards as the last thing they can do for the deceased. Others are unable to think clearly and rely heavily on family and friends to get them through. In this situation it is important that the help that is offered is not a well-meant takeover bid. 'Don't worry, leave it all to us' is not as helpful as it sounds because the chances are that things will be arranged in a way the bereaved would not have wished, which can lead to family stress and even bitterness in the future. The important thing is to be there, with much patience and understanding.

Denial and disbelief

In the first few days after bereavement, the child goes through a stage of being unable to accept that though someone has died they will not return.

Jamie, aged seven, knew that his father had died, but asked over and over again to come back to the hospice to see Dad, '...'cos he'll be waiting to see us'.

As with bereaved adults, children may think they hear the person's voice (a laugh . . .) or see them in the distance in the street.

Each time these incidents occur, it is another painful heart-rending reminder of the deceased, and part of a process which has to be gone through to come to a place of understanding and acceptance. This is a process which hurts and which is physically exhausting, yet brings tears of grief that are in themselves healing.

There is often a strong impulse to search – 'I can't help looking and listening for him everywhere'. Sometimes the bereaved travel many miles to return to places they think they might find them.

> 'I'm trying to find him . . .'
>
> 'Sometimes I think I see him at the end of the street or in a passing car – and follow – just in case.'

Although the bereaved adult knows it to be irrational behaviour intellectually, it takes much longer for the heart to know and accept.

> 'I cry out to him – "Where are you? Why did you leave me?"'

Meredith, aged fifteen, took the opposite approach:

> 'My sister cried all the time. I blocked it out of my head. I didn't want to think about it – I wanted to get on with my life.'

Small wonder that feelings of anger, frustration, emptiness and despair result when the search yields nothing. Anger may be directed at God for allowing it to happen, or at other people – the doctor, the hospital, the nurses, the family or even at the dead person for having apparently let them down.

Out of anxiety and fear there are moments of guilt, which feel very much the same. Moments when we wonder if we should have done it differently.

> 'If only … I'd spent more time with him.'
>
> 'If only … I'd been there when he died.'
>
> 'If only… I'd pressed for further treatment.'
>
> 'If only… I'd known what I know now.'

Alarm

Claudia Jewett writes:

> 'Because children look to their parents to keep them safe, the loss of a family member heightens their sense of vulnerability. Part of the shock of separation and loss is physical – caused by the sudden realisation of danger to oneself. Increased heart rate, muscular tension, sweating, dryness of mouth, frequent

> trips to the toilet, shortness of breath and/or deep sighing and rapid breathing, especially when talking about the lost person.
>
> These reactions come in waves, culminating in a general sense of weakness and exhaustion. As a result the child may be increasingly prone to infection – colds and tummy upsets, one after another. Children may pick at themselves, biting their nails, twiddling their hair and sometimes even pulling it out.'

These symptoms of stress may appear within the first 48 hours following the news of a loss or of a separation (as in divorce) or they may accompany significant anniversaries, holidays, a remarriage that makes the original parental reunion impossible, or an impending adoption finalization that makes the severance from the first family irreversible.

Acute grief

Yearning and pining

The wish for a different ending is strong: hope that somehow things will be different; that the person who has died will return. A great many children identify with those they see on TV and in films such as *Oliver* and *Annie* (loss and reunion) and will be moved to tears, both of joy for the fictional character and perhaps pain for their own hidden yearning.

This stage of grief recurs throughout life, in our wishes that a parent long dead could be there to see some accomplishment, new baby or marriage; or in the wish that a parental relationship could have been a closer one, even after we have accepted its imperfections. The conflict between the need to relinquish what has been lost and the wish to hold on to it – the pull between the past and the future – is the keynote to grief.

Searching

That which has been lost must be found and children set out to do just that. The fact that they can never succeed may build up into a feeling of fear, resulting in a restless, preoccupied child who is then very much afraid of losing other people: their grandparents, teacher, the family pet or a favourite toy.

Despair

Despair may follow when children realize that no amount of searching or longing is ever going to find the lost person.

They may tend to withdraw to cry, feeling that they cannot accept being loved by any other person. This is when, sometimes, 'school refusal' may occur. Despair can lead to depression.

Andrew, aged ten:

> 'It's like a black curtain swooping down and covering people in never-ending black.'

In circumstances of deep despair, for a child simply to be able to be with a person they love and trust can be a comfort in itself. They may instinctively look to that person for a reassuring cuddle – and take the initiative in doing so; or they may just want to be with them.

The adult, in responding, needs to be aware of two potentially conflicting issues in such a situation: the aching need of some but not all children for physical touch, for a warm cuddle; and the care that the adult needs to exercise to ensure that such a situation cannot be mis-read. Child protection procedures exist quite rightly to protect children from exploitation, but they have also affected the way some children perceive adults; they are less trusting. It is tragic that a child's natural need for comfort when they are in profound despair can now be coloured by the child not expressing that need for fear of 'abuse'. And the adult, equally longing to be comforting to the hurt child, becomes self-consciously aware of the alleged 'dangers' in doing so. In these circumstances a loving, reasonable and wise common sense needs to prevail.

What matters above all else is that the child knows that you, the adult, understand – and understand at a level that is beyond touch and beyond words. For a child to know that he or she is truly understood is a comfort and a healing in itself.

Anger

A child at any age, perhaps already feeling guilty, insecure and frightened by the loss, may be afraid to show angry feelings in case it makes things worse and drives away protective adults. The child becomes sullen, withdrawn and confused, because the anger is suppressed.

Bethany, aged eleven, said:

> 'I am not scared of dying, more of the pain it will expose others to. I suppose I say that because when my grandad died I felt the pain of losing someone, and I felt angry as if he'd died on purpose to upset me; then I felt guilty for feeling that.'

Anxiety and guilt

Children are strongly affected by the behaviour of those around them. When they see a sorrowing parent, or family members openly grieving, they may become anxious and feel that it must be their fault.

Nicole Krein writes:

> 'For instance, underlying conflicts about the birth of a new baby who subsequently dies may result in the surviving child feeling guilty and responsible for the baby's disappearance, and he may then fear that he too will die and disappear in his sleep. Sleep problems may become noticeable.'
>
> (*Clinical Paediatrics*, Vol. 18 No. 7, July 1979)

It is important for parents or professionals to clarify for children of this age that the baby has died of an illness which only affects some very young infants, not older children.

Pre-school children tend to experience their parents' preoccupation with grief as withdrawal of love from them. They may misbehave or cling to their parents at this time simply to get attention, feel secure and obtain reassurance that they are loved.

Signs of healing

The grief process is moving towards an end when there is:

i) painful acceptance of the reality of death;
ii) reorganization of life around the new circumstances;
iii) re-establishment of normal relationships and activities.

When these milestones are reached it shows that there has been much progress in coping with the bereavement.

Valerie, aged fifteen wrote:

> 'This one is for you, and then when I win at the dog show it's fun because I think he's watching me.'

4 Exploring people's needs

The needs of children

Children need information

Adults frequently say, 'It's the unknown that's the most difficult to deal with. The unknown frightens me . . . Tell me the truth. No matter how bad it is, it will be easier than not knowing'. Yet when it comes to children we assume that they prefer half-truths or even white lies, especially when facing something as difficult as death. If you watch them at play, however, you'll see that death and dying have quite significant roles ('Bang! Bang! You're dead'). Of course in play the 'dead' come to life again with remarkable and guaranteed frequency. It is equally true that while children can 'play' at death games, they find the real thing difficult – on the television news, for instance. Somehow we have to discover ways of helping them to come to terms with the reality of death.

Truth is of the essence here – truth given simply and clearly, accompanied by sympathy and support to bear it. In order for them to begin to understand, the information will have to be repeated more than once. (Can you take in bad news on first hearing?) They will need to be given opportunities and space to return to the subject in their own time and at their own pace – and that's a process, a process which may take weeks or months, or even years. 'Revisiting' in order to try to understand is the way we humans – including children – are made.

One of the special difficulties that children face is the concept of time. 'Today' is now; 'soon' is hours away; 'tomorrow' is years away. We have to be very careful not to foist adult ideas about time onto children who are almost literally time-less.

There is also the problem of trying to find the right words. It is perhaps wiser, though it requires great sensitivity, to allow the children to set the agenda. Their own explanations of what they understand about 'death' will help adults to find ways which link in to a child's way of thinking. Some parents once told me how their son, aged three and a half, faced with the sudden and totally unexpected death of his Grandma, said, 'Will Jesus be her little boy and open the door for her when she comes?'. They had no idea where their son had got these ideas from though they were a churchgoing family, but when he was given this opportunity to speak he found his own way of coping.

It is best to link any explanations of death to what the child knows about already, for instance the death and burial of a family pet or a dead bird. When a child comes up with one of those inevitable mind-bending questions, much will depend upon the beliefs and values of the adult who has been asked. Again, integrity and truth are of great importance. 'Where has Grandma gone?' will probably be answered by those with no Christian beliefs in terms of the life cycle, and how Grandma lives on in the minds and hearts of those who loved her. For Christians there will be answers based on beliefs about heaven and the new life promised through Jesus Christ. It is often the case, however, that adults launch into a theological description to answer a question when all the child really wants to know is, 'Which cemetery?'

Children need reassurance

Children do ask questions which to the onlooker appear straightforward, even blunt. They are not yet highly sophisticated in their use of language. 'Can I have my sister's toys now?' asked Helen, aged five. It is partly a straightforward request, partly a way of coming to terms with her own grief – even her own jealousy.

Practical questions abound. 'Who will take me to school? Who will give me my lunch money? Who will wash my games kit? Who will help me with my homework?'. These are not self-centred questions in any bad sense. They are 'landscape' questions: trying to restore familiar landmarks to the landscape so that order and value can be seen. The child needs to know what will change and what won't – and again those discussions need time to take place. They cannot be rushed.

Older children, less bothered by the social horrors of forgetting dinner money or whatever, may have questions on a wider time scale: 'What will I do in the school holidays? Shall I go to work? Shall I be able to go away to college?'. Such questions equally need time and care – they too are about landscape, only this time about prospective landscapes. We are helped to live by projecting forward in our imaginations in this way – and upon the death of a parent or sibling the prospective landscape may take as much of a hammering as the real one.

Younger children, on experiencing death, are also brought face to face with mortality. A world which had seemed safe, steady and reliable suddenly appears very unsafe, unsteady and wobbly.

They sometimes ask (and it takes much courage to ask this), 'Will you and I get ill and die now?'. It's a question which should not be ridiculed or laughed at; it begs for steady and reliable reassurance from the adults to whom they have turned to ask it.

One of the most frequent (but unspoken) fears that young children have is a sense of guilt. They feel that somehow they have been the cause of the death. Clearly the reassurance here ('So it isn't my fault then') will come as much from how you treat the child as from anything you say, but the compulsive desire of some young children to try to be perfect in order never to 'cause' another death (as they see it) needs much loving attention and care. It takes time to resolve.

Children need to express their feelings

Grief is not simply a matter of words. It's not expressed just in words; it's not answered just in words. Grief goes much deeper than that. Sometimes it is acted out in behaviour (not words) which can be unnerving for teachers and parents. There may be outbursts of anger and rage, swings of mood, withdrawal, looking 'lost'. All of these are normal – just as they are in bereaved adults. What is needed is a structure and an environment in which such powerful feelings can be expressed. Children need to know that anger is normal. They need to be assured that sadness does not last forever even though it can wash over us in waves, and we do not always know that the waves are coming.

How can feelings be expressed? A small child can play games or express feelings on a large sheet of paper with crayons and felt tips. An older child might want to do the same – or to write a story, or a letter to the dead person. None of this can or should be forced. As adults, we need to provide safe ways for them to express what they are unable to tell us in words.

They also need to be given permission to relax and have fun, to take part in body-stretching physical activities like football or running, or going for long walks with a gang of friends. These straightforward activities can in themselves be a wonderful release for anxiety and sadness and can help a child to let go of their feelings safely.

Another problem that children face relates to their own peer group. Althea, aged nine, said: 'It would help if your friends could just play with you and treat you like a normal person'. Adults cannot help here except to provide an example of 'normal treatment'.

Through the use of literature, teachers may explore the situation from another, less threatening angle; or they may find that they need to try to help the other children directly to understand what it is like for the one bereaved.

Undoubtedly one of the most important ways in which children cope with bereavement is through the use of 'treasures'. These may be insignificant to the adults ('You don't want that old watch . . . I'll get you a new one'), but to the child they have an almost sacramental significance. They are tokens of reassurance: signs that the person they loved really did exist; signs that, in spite of the worst that can happen, life does go on. Such mementoes, such treasures, belong to the child's own inviolate and secret world. As adults we ought not to trespass – but we should be aware that an object that seems to us meaningless and trivial may be priceless to the child. All we can do is to learn to be sensitive, and not to pry.

The needs of teenagers

It could be said that the upheaval of adolescence lies below the surface of each adult. Never more so than when we are coping with the grief that comes when someone close to us dies, and we are left feeling isolated and alone. The whole confusion of feelings akin to grief that haunts even the most normal teenager is once again ours. It's almost as if as adolescents we were grieving our childhood, or the ability to be like a child – our childishness; while at the same time longing to be grown up. I'm not entirely sure we ever completely leave behind the child in us, or quite achieve being grown up.

Well that's as may be: but for adolescents, and by that I mean children aged 11–14 through to 16, 17, 18, some younger some older, life isn't so easy. The trouble is that a lot of it is so subtle and uncomfortable that they can't quite see where it is coming from.

> 'Why does my Dad keep picking on me?'
>
> 'Why won't they let me stay out late?'
>
> 'Why do they always want to know where I am?'
>
> 'Why can't they just leave me alone?'

The struggle for independence and the search for a meaning to life and existence, gets muddled in with the need to be the same as their friends, the group, the gang. 'What the others think . . .' becomes paramount, and it's not until the 'grown-up' bit is reached that we have an inkling as to what it was all about – if then. At the time, 'life isn't fair' and 'parents are the pits'. Then one of them dies.

Many teenagers are caught between feeling unable to turn to the family they have been trying to break away from, and friends who do not know how to help them. Others will find themselves drawn back into the security that was always there, and will be able to talk with family members as a valued part of that family, experiencing the giving and receiving of care and openness which will stay with them always.

Jenny, aged sixteen

Jenny was a rebel amongst other things. She was the second sibling in a family of three daughters, and what she wanted more than anything else was to be like her apparently sophisticated older sister, as well as at times, her childish, often spoiled younger sister. This was mostly because she wasn't sure who Jenny was.

Things changed when her mother became ill. At first she didn't seem ill – just lethargic and uninterested. Then they noticed that her clothes didn't fit her as well as they used to; she was always meticulous about her appearance and they hated to see her hair looking lank and untidy and this once bright lady falling apart.

The older daughter was more interested in having a good time and hardly seemed to notice. Jenny the rebel gradually found herself looking after things at home in between her father going to work and her own school timetable. When her mother needed 'nursing' she was able to help the nurses and be there for her mother as well as for the rest of the family. Her profound maturity was not only of value to them then, but afterwards when her mother had died, she was grateful and pleased that she had been able to respond and give the support. That alone enabled her to overcome any feelings of guilt she may have had about her previous rebellious behaviour.

One of Jenny's problems was that she felt torn between staying at home to continue her role as 'woman of the house', and getting back to her studies and the life of a normal healthy seventeen-year-old. While it was necessary for each one of the family to adjust and do their fair share of the chores, it would not have been right to have taken advantage of her vulnerability at this point. It was her father who, with the help of friends, eased her back into her school and social activities. The mother role had in a sense been a refuge and a postponement of the teenage perspective of her own grief.

Happily her friends were mature enough to stand by and help her through some wobbly times. Sadly, this is not always the case. Adolescents are unpredictable and vulnerable. Many of them don't know how to give or receive comfort and may find themselves having to make jokes about death and funerals in order to deal with something beyond their understanding or experience.

Jenny's older sister Rachel became more preoccupied than ever with clothes and make-up. The family seldom saw her, she seemed to retreat into her headphones and loud and lengthy hours on the telephone; all of which heightened the already existing communication barrier between father and daughter which had sprung up even when her mother was still alive, and adolescence had seemed to be the cause. Over the following weeks and months she drank too much and her father suspected she had experimented with drugs. He, missing his wife particularly now, tried to imagine how she might have answered him – was this Rachel grieving for her mother yet unable to acknowledge it, or was this her own particular brand of adolescence? What was he to do? He felt some kind of discipline was called for but if so, what? How? He found talking to other bereaved parents helped, but realized there were no easy answers as to 'what to say' or 'what to do'. Her school work suffered as her attitude and behaviour continued to deteriorate; then came the anniversary of her mother's death and the floodgates opened. It came as a surprise to everyone, but it seemed as if only then, a year later, was she able to face the devastating reality of her mother's death. It was her form teacher to whom she turned and was able to talk freely, express her feelings, and that was the beginning of a different pain – the pain of healing.

Paul, aged fourteen

Paul's father died at home. The illness had progressed in fits and starts, daily raising and shattering their fragmented hopes. Within an already close family, Paul and his Dad were on the same wavelength. At the onset of the dreaded adolescence, Dad was almost always the one person who could avert the disasters, but when his illness made him too weak to cope, he was less and less able to cope with Paul.

Paul hated to see his father unable to help himself and couldn't bring himself to do things for him. The truth of it was he couldn't bear to see his father growing weaker each day; it hurt and frightened him in ways he couldn't explain. In order to push away the pain and deny the seriousness of the disease, he avoided being at home and spent more and more time with his friends, making believe his father wasn't sick at all. At least for a while he could forget about it and be himself. He wished it would end – not for his father to die but that the awfulness could finish.

I'm sure Paul's father knew what his son was feeling and why he was staying away. He would probably have told him, had he been able, that he loved him just the same, in spite of it, or even because of it.

When someone dies, friends and family often feel guilty about things they have said or done (or not done). In Paul's case he felt he knew he couldn't live up to the high standards he wanted to achieve for his father. In other words he'd failed; he'd let down his father, his family and himself. 'All that aggro! If I'd known it was going to end like this I wouldn't have given him such a hard time.' Would that it were so. The fact is that we would and frequently do.

Despite her own hurt his mother succeeded in keeping things at a practical level on a fairly even keel. She knew she would always be grateful to the network of friends and one or two family members who seemed to know when things at home were a bit bumpy. By their 'being there' over a cup of coffee and sharing and listening and enabling her to talk, she knew and felt support. So when Paul got into a fight at school, or went through periods of unusual quiet and apparent depression, her support network was able to reassure her that this was normal.

Adolescents hide their emotions as best they can for fear of being seen to be different by their peers; inevitably there are outbursts of anger, boredom, sadness and crying. We are none of us prepared for the length of time grief takes, and that it comes and goes like waves on the shore.

Like most of us Paul and his mother found the anniversaries almost too powerful to handle. Grief is revisited on birthdays, at Christmas, at times that have been special, and on the anniversary of the death. The first of each of these was the worst but they got through as best they could and found that they were able at these times to begin to share their thoughts and feelings with each other, as well as the memories.

Paul gradually settled to life without his father. He reverted to bringing his friends home and was chosen for the football team. 'Dad would have been pleased,' he said. So the healing had begun; and although life would never be the same as before, Paul was coping with life and with death, and there was light, albeit a different light, at the end of that very long tunnel.

The needs of parents

The need for information

One of the most difficult questions which any teacher, minister or friend can be asked is, 'What should I tell the children?' The answer depends so much on the age and background of the child. Sometimes, indeed, the question is a kind of camouflage which might be better expressed as: 'Help me to make sense of this for myself, so that I can then help my children'. When the question is asked you will need to be prepared – not only by knowing hard information, but also because you have wrestled with the reality of death and have made some kind of sense of it for yourself.

Claudia Jewett writes:

> 'The two most important things to tell the child are, first that the dead person will never return and, second, that the person's body is to be buried in the ground, or burned to ashes and then buried.'

That may seem stark – and if the child were told in that way it would indeed be hard; but essentially what Claudia Jewett is pleading for is a sense of the real. As Peter Gould, Chaplain of Basingstoke Hospital, says: 'Reality is not something to face but to go through'.

The reality of death, however, includes the physical facts: cessation of life, burial, irreversibility. It also includes the emotions of those involved. Children are brilliant and subtle at picking up the emotions around them – tension, tiredness, breaks in routine. Body language conveys so much to them – they learn to read its meaning long before they learn words. No amount of silence or secrecy can hide the fact that something is wrong. Overheard conversations, sometimes misunderstood, or one-sided telephone calls whispered or cut short as they enter the room – all make the child fearful and ready to draw his or her own worrying conclusions.

The child needs to be included, as far as possible, in the whole event – in the shared shock, the explosions of grief, the corporate attempt to make sense of things. As educator and author Eda Le Shan writes:

> 'A child can live through anything so long as he is told the truth and is allowed to share with loved ones the natural feelings people have when they are suffering.'

While the parents are asking, 'What should I tell them?', the chances are that the child has already begun to try to make sense of the new situation. Parents need to be encouraged to be truthful – both in their words and in their feelings. There will be some resistance to this from family, friends and the neighbourhood. They may say, 'Children are too young to understand'. The fact is that from a very early age children are constructing 'understanding' of the world – and that understanding, to be complete, must involve death. Naturally our words and actions have to be chosen to suit the age of the child but, again, children will often set their own agendas, provided that the adults are prepared to listen and to take their questions seriously, no matter how quaintly phrased.

Parents who have strong religious beliefs may couch the answers in the language of their own faith-community and that can be very helpful. It is possible, however, for such answers to be given before the child has, as it were, asked the question – or be given in such a way that the child knows that the real question has been evaded. This is not a simple situation and it is not cut and dried.

Perhaps parents need encouragement most of all to see that children 'revisit' the questions from time to time and make sense of them in new ways. Understanding is a process, not the provision of pat answers.

The need for reassurance

Perhaps the best way to help parents is to show that you are willing to be there for them. It's a kind of act of solidarity – a solidarity built on shared human experience, on shared vulnerability and on shared strength. They will need to talk through their own feelings of anxiety – about themselves, about their ability to cope (that's the 'What shall I tell them?' syndrome again), and about their own reactions. For the parents it might well be their own first encounter with death – so their struggle is twofold; they are trying to cope themselves and in their own flounderings are trying to help their children as well. Not easy. Their bewilderment needs to be acknowledged and accepted.

Some of the reassurance can be of a plainly practical kind: asking them, for instance, if they would like to be put in touch with one of their local clergy or a social worker, or with others who have been through similar experiences. They might need help in sorting out how to arrange the funeral; get them to contact a minister or a funeral director. They may need help with catering, with washing clothes and so on. If the parents are on their own in the locality (their own families may live hundreds of miles away), a school or church, if appropriate, can organize a network of help and support which can be invaluable.

Agencies in the area will be able to give help and advice; the Citizens Advice Bureau, for instance, or a local hospice. But parents also need to be encouraged to see that some of the reassurance and the understanding can come from deep within their own personalities. There is an understandable tendency to look to experts, especially in a crisis. That should not be at the expense of losing confidence in one's own ability to learn – and some of that confidence comes from a willingness to make mistakes and to learn from them.

From time to time, a parent or teacher will feel the need to involve a professional counsellor. Perhaps there is a real problem and the child's behaviour is proving difficult to handle. Telephone numbers of various helpful and informed agencies may be found in Appendix B, pages 67-9.

The need to express feelings

There have been many changes in the way our society conducts itself. The way in which we express our feelings of grief no longer has the support of an acknowledged and public set of rules. At one time everyone wore black; the curtains of the house were kept drawn shut; people in the street stood still as the hearse went past and men took their hats off. Most of those public customs for a private family funeral have disappeared, seen only on very special occasions for royalty, public figures or celebrities. Carpets of flowers and toys appeared after the death of Diana. Crowds lined the route to say goodbye to the Queen Mother. When a child was killed, flowers and teddy bears were laid outside the school and local church. But the expression of private grief in public is still rare. This can leave grieving parents in even greater bewilderment. Inside they may feel bleak, lost and desperate, but there are no outward signs to show that this is the case – either through special clothes or special rituals. As a result the public expression of grief is driven underground, and the theatre of grief is driven inwards.

With such changes has come a sense of bewilderment about feelings aroused by grief. A woman wearing black and looking gaunt and exhausted will be asked if she is ill. No matter what has happened to the public rules of mourning, the feelings of the bereaved remain the same, feelings which are immensely powerful and disturbing. To be able to provide a forum where those feelings may be expressed and learnt from is a great privilege – it may be one which you, your school or church can and should provide.

5 The big dyings

Death of a parent

The biggest blow any child can suffer is to lose its mother or father; that which had provided solace and stability is no longer there. The patterns have broken and can never be reassembled in exactly the same form again. Someone described it in another way:

> 'It's like an aeroplane. The family needs both sets of wings to fly successfully. Of course, one wing is left, but the plane is thrown off balance, stability temporarily disappears . . .'.

Children in such circumstances can try to restore the balance: girls by trying to become the perfect 'mother', boys by trying to become the perfect 'father'. This can be acceptable for a while (it's their way of coping), but it should not be taken for granted nor become the norm. Children need to be children and childhood cannot be submerged under quasi-adult roles. They have to be gradually eased out of the substitute-parent model and rediscover their own childhood and their own needs. Children who carry the role for a very long time may find it particularly hard to readjust if the surviving parent wishes to remarry, or even to adjust to their own possible marriage. In such circumstances professional guidance may be necessary.

What of the strong feelings aroused by the death of parents? There is often considerable anger directed inwardly by the child against itself or sometimes outwardly to the parent who has died: 'How could you leave me like this?' Often this is accompanied by a subsequent backwash of guilt.

The anger needs to be accepted as a normal, inevitable part of the grieving process – but more than that, as an expression of real feelings. The denial of such feelings by well-meaning adults – 'You shouldn't say that…' – is not always right or appropriate.

With anger may also come a sense of self-pity and because children are brilliant manipulators and actors, they can use their self-pity to their own advantage. 'I'll be allowed to have that (so I'll ask for it) because people feel sorry for me.' Self-pity is a natural feeling – it is truly dreadful to be bereaved of a parent – but while it's natural it must not be allowed to dominate all other expressions of grief. This may take a long while to understand.

It is also the case that the parent who has died becomes 'idealized'. They were the perfect mother, the perfect father. Look at memorial stones in graveyards for the real mixture of good and bad which makes up each of us – and you will not find it. Graveyards, ironically, epitomize the triumph of hope over experience, of ideal over actual. It takes a while for the reality of the parent to be allowed room in the child's mind – partly because to allow it (though it must take place) is to acknowledge the finality of the separation. Real people do die.

Anger, depression, idealization, grief – all of these are part of the bereavement journey; but they are only part of the journey, not the destination. Each of them needs to be stopped at and, in a sense, experienced before the journey can continue. It is the function of teachers, clergy and friends in such circumstances to stay with the child at each of the stages but, without haste, also to encourage the child to move on. That is done only by sensitivity and solidarity and learning to trust oneself and one's own insights and uncertainties. There is no magic wand to make sure that it all goes right, just as there is no perfect way to grieve and no perfect way to have got to the place where grieving becomes built in to the way we think and feel, where it becomes a resource and not a burden.

Peggy, aged eleven:

> 'I can't grasp the fact that my dad is lying there under the ground. I think of him more as a ghost-like person floating around everywhere.'

Death of a grandparent

Children usually share a comfortable, relaxed and close relationship with their grandparents. They are people who are 'good to be with'. One-parent or divorced families often depend heavily on a grandparent to provide stability for the children. This is especially so if their being there enables a lone parent to go out to work. Even if this is not the case, when a grandparent dies, children learn a lot from the way in which their own parents share their feelings and cope.

Mourning is a learned experience. Sadly it is often at this point that parents want to 'protect' their children. Sometimes they don't even tell them of the death until after the funeral. Is this not in fact their inability to share and cope? In so doing they are actually shutting the children out and depriving them of an important part of life.

Children need and understand mementos. Something to remember could be given to them, or they could choose something that had a particular association. It could be unexpected – a photograph, a set of tools, a watch, or even an old jersey: ''Cos if I shut my eyes I can feel Grandpa there'.

Death of a brother or sister

The death of a child at any age is the worst thing imaginable for any parent. It is the most painful and least acceptable of any loss, not least because it upsets the natural order of things. It is, quite simply, the wrong way round.

In the ensuing and understandable rush of sympathy and deep concern that flows in on all sides for the parents, it is likely that the sorrowing child may be accidentally forgotten. It must be remembered that the child too has lost a baby brother or sister; the big sister or brother they turned to when they needed someone to talk to; the brother they fought and argued with every day but who remained their best friend. The one with whom they shared a bedroom is never coming home.

Parents' reactions are usually supportive but, particularly in the case of sudden death, there is the risk of the surviving child being forgotten, resented or shut out. The result is that the child feels he or she is to blame.

If the parents blame God for 'taking the child' insecurity sets in as the survivor waits to be taken as well.

In moments of intense anguish, when parents have nothing left to give in the way of emotional support, their distress has been known to drive them to say, 'you killed her'. This leaves what can be a lifelong sense of misunderstanding and rejection unless it is handled very carefully and wisely by someone outside the family circle who is aware of the problem. Such a comment can be desperately hurtful, partly because it may chime in with what the surviving child has thought: 'Perhaps if I'd not done . . . Perhaps if I'd not said…'. Their undue, but understandable, sense of responsibility can lead them into all kinds of unhappiness.

The surviving child needs to be assured that he or she does not have to be 'two' children; that is, the child is itself and must not try to be its dead brother or sister as well. This can be terribly difficult because in order to regain (as the child sees it) parental approval he or she may want to become, as it were, the dead child.

The reality and lovability of the surviving child need to be constantly borne in mind by those offering pastoral care. Such children deserve to be given their own time, and space, for their own particular needs and fears.

Death of a friend

Friends affirm and trust each other, so the loss of a friend can be a huge blow.

At different ages friendship means different things. To the pre-school child, a friend is a playmate; to the child of school age, a confidant who can share secrets, thoughts and feelings, and a companion in school and on outings.

Teachers should be aware of the loneliness and isolation felt by a particular child following the death of a friend, and also by the rest of the class to whom, although perhaps not so 'special', he or she was a comrade and part of the group. The children feel vulnerable and insecure – part of the jigsaw has been lost – they feel incomplete. They need encouragement to talk about their feelings and these, no matter how bizarre, need to be acknowledged.

Death of a family pet

To young and old alike a much-loved pet is very much part of the family: a friend, a confidant, and a source of joy and comfort, particularly when things aren't going so well.

The death of a pet can be devastating, particularly to an adolescent child who may feel that the family dog was the only one who ever understood or listened.

It is often through the death of a pet that children first experience grief, and with just as much pain as if an adult dies. This is why it is often wise to wait a while before replacing a dead animal, so that the child has time to work through his or her feelings and learn a little of what life and death are all about.

6 Terminal illness

Death at home

Provided that the conditions are right and that the family can cope, the best place to die is at home. Having said that, it is not always appropriate.

Much is to be gained from openly sharing and honestly talking with the children about what is happening. It is a good idea to set aside times in the day when the family can be together, relaxed over a cup of tea, or a drink in the evening – going over the day's events, what the doctor said, looking into the future and reminiscing about the past. Poignant, close, sad, funny times – and golden memories afterwards.

Constant telephone enquiries and visitors to the house can become almost an intrusion and there is a risk of children feeling left out. They need specific chores to do and for which they are responsible, as part of a carefully ordered routine, in order to feel that, despite everything, their world is not collapsing around them.

It is also important that the illness is not allowed totally to disrupt or take over the household. Family carers have to recharge their batteries and children need to let off steam. As well as this the patient too needs privacy and space for his or her own adjustment and letting go. Emotional pain is exhausting. Time out on the heath for partner and children should be seen as a positive response to the need to be 'normal', to relax and enjoy leisure, in some way to begin to adjust to how life will be after the other partner has died.

Dying in a hospice or hospital

Dying sometimes takes a long time. A long protracted illness, resulting in sleepless nights and a shattered family, needs professional help. A hospice helps to take care of the entire family, sharing their individual needs and fears and enabling them to stay alongside and support one another and the children, as well as the patient. The role of the hospice team is the same as for the minister, teacher or friend, to facilitate the parents to support and understand their children, being careful not to professionalize everything. The awareness that there are people who care will help to carry a distraught father or mother and see them through with enough strength to be able in turn to help their children.

As at home, the routine, keeping things as normal as possible by continuing to do the things they would normally do, is important. At the same time parents should be aware that children may well begin to do things they would not normally do or have grown out of, like bed-wetting, or nail-biting. This will probably happen only once or twice; usually it will pass but, if not, professional help may be necessary.

A small child may need the reassurance of a light left on at night – and why not? Or the child may wake up in the night and seek the security of the parental bed. So long as, once asleep, the child can be slipped back into his or her own bed to wake up there in the morning, no harm will have been done and probably both will have been comforted.

Protecting a child by 'letting him remember his mother as she was' is not always a good idea. A child's imagination knows no bounds; terrifying fantasies can be worse than anything it will ever see, which might be weight loss, hair loss or a Mum apparently asleep, free of pain and comfortable. A child either doesn't notice or doesn't mind physical changes and certainly needs the reassurance of knowing that she is there and 'all right'.

Hospital visiting isn't easy. A small child cannot sit still and quiet for long; an older child feels self-conscious. Often there is lack of privacy; sustained conversation can be a strain. Actions speak louder than words. The reason behind a reluctance or even refusal to visit is most likely that the child is frightened of what they may find there or of not knowing what to say.

It helps children if they can be useful – arranging flowers, rearranging the cards, making drawings (this helps to express feeling too). They could be encouraged to take some homework or something made at school to show Mum or Dad. The hospital may have a TV room or quiet room, so that the child can come and go and relax during the visit. Children should be encouraged to talk about people, places, things that are familiar – all the domestic details that will be reassuring to the dying patient too.

7 Sudden death

Who should tell the child?

> 'I knew something was wrong when I was called to the headmaster's office. He put his hands on my shoulders and said, "Your father has been killed in a car accident, your Mum will be here shortly – she's coming with a friend so that you can all go home together."'

In this case Helen's home was a long way from school so it fell to the headmaster to tell her, clearly and directly, knowing that when her mother arrived she would be able to repeat and thus confirm the news. When a parent dies suddenly it is best that a loving and close member of the family or family friend, but preferably the surviving parent, breaks the news.

In Helen's case the headmaster did the right thing in giving her the facts as soon as possible and making sure that her mother was on the way to school to confirm what had happened and to be with her daughter. This way Helen could be in no doubt as to what had happened, and felt herself to be a trusted part of the family group. The principle is to give the information straight away from a reliable source, and then to reunite the child and the surviving parent as soon as possible. When news is given by a stranger there is a tendency not to believe it.

Tim's young mother had only an hour between receiving the news from the police and the time when the school run was due home. An hour in which to struggle with her own shock, and try to think how best to cope with seeing and telling Tim that his father had died. She knew she had to tell him straight away, to tell him as calmly and as clearly as possible that 'Daddy had died in an accident at work'. She wasn't sure how he would react – he might be angry, he might not react or hardly at all at first, and that would be hard, but he might cry which would be her undoing. If he asked questions how was she going to answer them – she probably didn't know the answers.

In the event Tim knew immediately that his mum was upset. 'What's up Mum?' They sat down together by the sitting-room fire and she told him slowly and painfully that a part of the machine that Daddy had been working on had broken loose and fallen on top of him and killed him. Tim needed to know if his father would come home. He said he wished they hadn't let him go to work that day and his mother took great care to reassure him that the accident had not happened because they had let him go to work; it was none of it their fault.

'And so what will we do now?' Tim asked. His mother tried to be as positive as she could, reassuring him that they would stay in their house, that she would always be there, that his grandparents would be very much around and that Tim would go back to school after the funeral. They sat and cried a bit and talked some more, and then Tim realized his father wouldn't be at the football on Saturday and his mother just hugged him and said 'No'.

Most young children seem to have some form of extrasensory perception. They may not know the facts yet but they know when something is wrong and if they are being isolated from it. Protection then begins to feel like rejection. Some grown-ups avoid talking to children about their loss because they can see that it will take them much too close to their own past losses, separations or rejections. As a result the children feel afraid and muddled and want someone who can talk to them.

We can best help a children like Tim by giving them time and space and encouraging them to talk about their own feelings. In our nervousness and anxiety to get it right for them, and say the things we've worked out as being important, we grown-ups usually talk far too much. Their heads are probably buzzing with questions which they can't bring themselves to ask and they can't get a word in edgeways. It sometimes helps to get at the questions with a touch of humour, even black humour. 'Wasn't it awful when...?' or 'Did you see...?' If they do manage a question, say on 'death' or 'heaven' or 'soul', and that's beyond you, then be honest. If that means saying, 'I don't know', they will respect you for it. Maybe that's a point at which a teacher, the vicar, a relative or a friend can be asked to help.

In areas where the surviving parent has difficulty others can sometimes cope superbly well, not necessarily better but differently. The parent too will need a confidant to whom they can express their own adult grief so that they don't come to depend on the bereaved child to shoulder their loneliness. Both child and adult need to grieve in their own way and in their own time.

Memories

Tim needs to remember and be encouraged to talk about his father who has died – to look at his photograph and remember the good times – the football match when Tim scored his first goal and how proud his father was of him, and not only then. For some reason we're not always very good at telling our own children how proud of them we really are – sometimes it takes someone else to do it for us – someone who knows us as well as the child. A child is helped by being made aware of how our memories can be a comfort to us and help us to feel stronger, even or especially at our darkest moments.

Will we see him again?

Tim and his mum and one of her close friends went to say goodbye to his father in the Chapel of Rest at the local undertakers. Some members of the family didn't think it was a good idea, but his mother felt that she had to let Tim see that although his father was dead, he was, in a sense, all right. She had checked it out with the undertaker first. There were no outward signs that his father had been hurt. He was in fact dressed in pyjamas.

At first Tim didn't say anything, then, 'You can see he's not breathing . . . he is very quiet . . . he's not moving . . . he's not usually that quiet when he's asleep but he does look comfy.' Tim had drawn a picture which he laid beside his father and both he and his mother seemed reassured by that and by the stillness and general sense of peace.

Saying goodbye

It is important that Tim is included in the funeral or the memorial service. It is here that he will have the chance to see that a change really has taken place, that other people want to say goodbye and that they too are affected and share his sadness and want to support him as part of a grieving family. To leave him out is to make him feel uneasy, isolated and rejected. Tim's mother was sensitive to that. She also knew that although her loss was different to his, her responses and her ability to cope, and even sometimes not to cope, would somehow set an example for him in as much as she had openly expressed her thoughts and feelings and enabled him to do the same – to have his first glimpse as to what death was all about.

A few weeks later she was not too surprised to find a drawing of a coffin and a funeral, to be followed by Tim and his chums acting out 'funerals'. She'd been told to expect something of the kind – that it was normal for children to come to terms with events that happen in this way, and that maybe there would be more questions at bedtime.

8 Suicide

To condense such an emotive subject into a relatively small space takes us straight to the heart of the matter. What does a child feel when struck by the impact of knowing that a parent has ended his or her life?

There is no warning. There can be no preparation as there can be when someone has been ill, and therefore no goodbyes. Furthermore, unlike a sudden heart attack or a road accident where death happened, this death was made to happen.

Most very young children cannot appreciate the significance of suicide but there are some who undoubtedly can, and bring to it questions that require an answer.

A child's view of suicide

A *view* is usually something contained and organized, so it might be more relevant and accurate to use the word *nightmare*. Thoughts and questions abound:

> Why?
>
> How could she?
>
> It must have been my fault…
>
> Did he really love me?
>
> She's left us – she's gone without a thought or a goodbye.
>
> Nothing . . . a mess.
>
> He didn't want us.
>
> Was it my fault?
>
> What did I do that was so wrong? or I shouldn't have…
>
> Did he think about us?
>
> I'm not loveable.

> I wasn't worth her staying.
>
> I didn't live up to his expectations.
>
> I can't think straight, it doesn't make sense.

Some children may not be able to face it at all. As well as guilty feelings and blaming oneself and probably other survivors too, suspicion sets in. There may have been something he or she couldn't talk about – terminal illness, redundancy, a sexual problem, depression, an unhappy marriage, a failed relationship.

In families where there has been a history of alcoholism, depression or sexual abuse, to a certain degree there will be feelings of relief that those things are gone, but guilt and remorse soon step in to fill the gap.

Fear that the surviving parent will take the same drastic step causes insecurity and mistrust, and later on in life – 'Will I do the same?'

More nightmare thoughts:

> What did he go through to make him kill himself?
>
> Did it hurt?
>
> Did she really mean to go that far?
>
> Was it meant to be a cry for help that was only supposed to frighten us and it went too far?
>
> Could we have stopped him or her if we'd known or even realized?
>
> I should have known, but would it have made a difference and did he just want to die?

The implications for a surviving spouse are many and hard to bear. Small wonder that they may choose not to face it – for a while at least – let alone sit down and talk it through with their child. At times like these, thank goodness for all the relations, friends and good neighbours who can 'be there', each in their own way with something invaluable to offer – their loving concern and their time.

Again, in principle the best person to tell a child is the surviving parent. They may not be able to face doing that, or at least not alone and without your moral support. Or they may ask you to take the lead while their response is to hold the child on their knee while you gently explain what has happened. That way the child receives the information given in your words as well as the warmth, comfort, love, reassurance and trust from the parent.

When they are feeling stronger, they will cope without you, for the moment they both need you. The child will give the cues for you to follow. One danger is that the parent will have expectations as to the right way for the child to react. It is hard for them to let the child express strong feelings of anger, sadness and despair; you will need to be the one who listens and accepts and is non-judgemental. It will settle – for a while at least – until the feelings are worked through. As the child grows in years, so the questions change in line with their ability to understand.

Different forms of reaction and grief

> 'I see it now…I never knew how my mother died; my father wouldn't/couldn't talk about her. There seemed to be a sort of conspiracy of silence and when the family got together I used to dread her name being mentioned. Even though I wanted to talk about her they just used to change the subject, and when I asked my grandparents or my aunt about her they just went quiet, or avoided giving me a straight answer – but their eyes gave them away. Years later, on the verge of leaving home to get married, I had to know the truth. Out of the blue I asked him; he was taken by surprise and said, "She overdosed."
>
> Funny thing really. We talked and talked for ages – you know how you can sometimes. We had the sort of conversation we'd never been able to have before. Now that it was out in the open it was such a relief.
>
> My father couldn't talk about it at the time – it was his way of coping. Left to his own devices and given time he probably would have done so, but there was a lot of family pressure around; he said his sister had told him she had thought he didn't care about my mother's death because he never talked about her or grieved openly for her. She on the other hand

> cried a lot and wanted to talk. They reacted completely differently, but they were doing it their own way.
>
> Dad said Mum would understand and that was what really mattered, but he wishes now he'd told me sooner and saved me a lot of unhappiness – he can see it now.'

Blame within the family

> 'Before my father died we used to see a lot of my grandparents, but after that we never saw them. I found out later they blamed my Mum and me for what happened . . .'

A family, made up of individuals, struggles to come to terms with the stigma of suicide, as well as with the loss and what that means to each of the different relationships.

Bereavement, loss – whatever word we use it hurts. Being angry is a way of expressing that pain, directed at self, relatives, friends and probably the doctor. They are all potential targets. From the depths of our own darkness, we hear, 'It's all your fault – you killed her'.

Support from outside the home – family members, friends, the vicar, the doctor – can prevent the temporary resentment and potential violence from taking a hold and spilling over to frighten the children. We all need space for our grief. Someone to cry to and cry with. Someone who will listen and walk alongside, or take the children to the park so that they can take it out on a football.

Does suicide run in families?

> 'It's ironic really – my father committed suicide when I was fourteen years old. He'd had trouble in his last job – couldn't take the pressure and the travelling – eventually it got too much for him and he put an end to it all by shooting himself.
>
> Now thirty years later I'm in a company that's having to make people redundant left, right and centre; it could be my turn any day – how will I cope? "Will I cope at all?" is the question that

> bothers me most. I'm aware of the family history, although they say that just because the generation before died that way it doesn't mean the one that follows will do the same – but family patterns and all that? You never know do you?'

There is no conclusive evidence that suicide runs in families, or that it is inherited or will recur in the surviving children. But family patterns can be quite powerful and it is understandable that the question is asked, especially when people say things like '. . . and you are so like your father'.

Children may not worry about this aspect so much at the time of the death as later on in adult life. When a parent commits suicide most children will be more concerned that their parent didn't love them any more, or that they had done something so naughty it had made them do it.

The truth, the whole truth

> 'My Mum hanged herself. My brother was six and I was nine. Dad told us when the vicar came round just before the funeral. It didn't make much sense then. He said we'd be bound to hear it from somebody else, and he'd rather it was from him.
>
> We didn't understand what suicide was. The vicar said it meant taking your own life and that sometimes people choose to make themselves die. Dad said, "He means she killed herself."
>
> Up to that point I'd never seen my father cry – my mother used to cry a lot I remember, but never my father. He kept hugging us and saying he was sorry. He was in a terrible state. We were looked after by the lady next door. We'd find things in the fridge for our tea, and she'd be there when we got home from school. It all seems a bit vague now. But I will never forget Dad's words – "She killed herself." It was like learning a new language; we heard the words but didn't understand what they meant until later, and then I remember feeling so ashamed, as if it was my fault. It wasn't, of course, but it took a long time to believe it for myself.'

9 The school community and tragic events

The school community can be one of the key sources of support for a bereaved child. However, staff may themselves need support and training in how best to help such children.

All schools will also be directly affected from time to time by tragic events, such as the death of a member of the school community. Then there are the tragic events on a national and international scale, such as 11 September or the abduction and murder of a child; most children will have no personal involvement in such events but are nonetheless affected by them. This chapter provides basic advice to both teachers and parents on supporting children in the aftermath of such events.

Preparing children to cope with death and bereavement

From primary school upwards, teachers can and should introduce death as part of children's early training for everyday life. There are books that illustrate nature as the seasons change, flowers bloom, wither and die. Trees come to life again in the spring, leaves fall in the autumn to make room for the cycle to repeat. Families have pets and many a hamster or gerbil is the pride and joy of a primary school classroom. My children's school was no exception. When the hamster died, one little girl was distraught. It was a sharp learning curve for all of us. He was laid in a grass-filled box and buried in a quiet corner of the school compound under a tree. That corner was turned into a flower garden cared for by the children and their teacher in their lunch breaks. In class the children made drawings and paintings and wrote their own stories about him. In talking about him and realizing his value, sadness seemed easier to bear and accept.

Supporting a bereaved child in school

The child who needs to talk is unlikely to do so in a busy classroom. The teacher should make a quieter time and place available when he or she is able to listen and answer questions, and encourage the child to talk about the person who has died. The child needs to be reassured that the teacher will be there to give help whenever she or he can.

It is worth remembering that the feelings of grief are uncharted territory to children and perhaps even to some younger teachers who may not have experienced the death of someone close to them.

No one should be surprised at or critical of a child's honesty. He or she may express the strangest fears and concerns that may shock. Moments like this should be seen as an opportunity to talk about what and how they are feeling.

Children are naturally fun-loving. Play in itself is good for hearts and minds as well as being a release from tension and anxiety. It can be the beginning of 'letting go' of their grief but makes some children feel guilty that they have laughed and enjoyed themselves. They need to be reassured that the person they remember would be happy to see them having fun.

Children are resilient. 'Being there' for a child and seeing that child respond positively is a privilege and one not to be taken lightly or without care.

An event that affects the school community: breaking the news

Most schools will be affected by tragic events from time to time, even if they do not reach the national consciousness.

When a shocking event takes place that affects a school community it is the staff as well as the pupils that need support. If a relationship of trust has been built up with local ministers then it is very good practice to ask one of them to come and be with the school community. They can then support the staff as the staff support the students.

The way in which information is given depends to some extent on the age of the children. Young children usually benefit from staying in small and familiar settings (the classroom) with their own teachers. A judgement can then be made as to whether the class teacher is capable of breaking the news and dealing with the emotions that arise, or whether the headteacher or other members of the senior management team should move from class to class.

For older children a series of year group assemblies following one after another is often appropriate leaving them to return to their forms but with the recognition that they may need time then to assimilate the information before being able to continue with the day's work. This will depend to some extent on how well they know the person or people involved in the tragedy.

Reactions to tragic events: a primary school on 11 September 2001

Children and staff alike heard of the terrible events in New York from shocked parents at the school gates. Parents feeling the need to be near and see their children safe, wanted to get home and check on the whereabouts of family and close friends.

The following morning each form teacher, uncertain how much the children would have understood of what they had seen on TV or heard being talked about at home, gathered their own class to talk about what had happened all that distance away in New York.

Mostly the children were aware of what had happened but, as this was the start of the school year, were probably more taken up with getting into the school routine and finding their friends.

But they knew that 'aeroplanes had driven into two big high towers and lots of people had got killed'.

Later, the headteacher, in a special assembly, addressed the whole school and was able to acknowledge what had happened: that lots of people had been killed in New York. She went on to say: 'We all feel sad as we remember those who have died in New York; those who have been hurt, and those who have lost family and friends they loved'. Afterwards the children talked about what had they seen and heard with each other and with their teachers, even if they were unable to understand or articulate the full meaning of it all.

The importance of encouraging communication and openness in response to a situation like this cannot be overstated: parents need to feel confident that, in a crisis, the school has the interests of their children at heart and will respond to such crises with common sense and sensitivity, in partnership with parents, to ensure that the message and support given is along the same lines. As with families, there may be many different 'cultures' and differing points of view within a school and, where possible, other approaches to tackling such difficult areas should be taken into account.

Young children tend to 'puddlejump' with feelings and activities, in other words their brokenheartedness can change amazingly quickly into lighthearted joy. Likewise, they leap from one activity to another as their concentration allows. So in their response to the events of 11 September, although the overall feeling was one of sadness, young children were able to turn, move on and get on with their day because they had no direct involvement in the event and that is how five- and six-year-olds react to most things.

Later, the children would come back to the event and respond, as this age group often does, with graphic drawings, in this case of flaming towers and lopsided planes.

Secondary school reactions to tragic events

With such a major event as 11 September 2001 children usually have little or no personal involvement beyond the images they see and the public commentary. A year on from 11 September 2001, a group of children aged between eleven and fifteen attending a secondary school in Surrey were asked to recall how they had felt about the events of that day:

Grant, aged 11, tried to rationalize what had happened:

> 'It was a cruel thing to do, but they only do it because they are sick and selfish.'

Most of the children were still outraged, or used language that indicated that they had felt outraged, but were beginning to temper their response. Adults and children alike had watched repeatedly on TV in horror as the planes hit and the towers collapsed; none of us could believe that what we were seeing was real.

Natalie, aged 15, felt a sense of injustice and disbelief:

> 'It was like something you saw in a film, but this *was* real, and that shook me up inside... I kept asking myself, how can any human being treat another with no care at all? No care about

> whether they live or die, no care about how many families they destroy.'

It took a while for reality to strike home: that suicide bombers have no boundaries, that we are all vulnerable.

Stuart, aged 12, expressed a sense of helplessness, sadness and anger:

> 'Scared of what might happen next, sad for all the families that have been affected, angry that it all happened. I want to do something about it, but there is nothing much I can do.'

Children were undoubtedly touched, and the more imaginative and sensitive the older children were, the better they were at imagining themselves in that scenario. At the time it was hard to escape from the last recorded telephone messages from the planes and the images that bombarded us from our TV screens. There is no question that if we become parents and grandparents ourselves, we are fearful for our children.

Those of us with an inbuilt fear of flying in planes have for years imagined bumping into buildings and mountain sides; this event not only confirmed but capped our worst fears. My feeling is that as adults wobbled, our children picked up some of our insecurity.

Paul, aged 15, felt fearful and insecure:

> 'My father was in Australia on September 11th. I remember just wanting him home, and wanting my family to be somewhere safe.'

Douglas, aged 10, was in France with his school on 11 September:

> 'I wasn't aware of the implications until my mum was so pleased to get me back home, and I began to understand . . .'

For others, a tragic event of this kind may trigger memories of an earlier, perhaps unresolved loss. Teachers and carers should be aware of and sensitive to this: a child's reaction may be out of all proportion to their actual experience or involvement in it.

Jack, aged 12, was able to relate to his already existing grief after his much-loved grandparents had died suddenly:

> 'It's just that I never got to say goodbye to them because they died so suddenly – that is what most shocks and worries me.'

The impact of a tragic event nearer home

Many schools will be affected by tragic events from time to time. Sadly, road traffic accidents, rail crashes, suicides and fatal illnesses happen. However, the abduction and murder of children, such as those of Holly Wells and Jessica Chapman at Soham, Cambridgehsire, in 2001, seems to touch something different.

Children get used to their contemporaries moving away to different schools or other parts of their country. Holly and Jessica 'went away' with no possibility of returning. Their close friends and children in their class showed a level of bereavement that was palpable. They missed them, and as with any other loss of someone close, their grief may have left them feeling confused and bewildered, with outbursts of tears and irritability; they may have shown anxiety at being separated from parents; difficulty going to sleep and perhaps fear of the dark and of having nightmares. They will have felt vulnerable for a while, afraid something of the same could happen to them – feeling jumpy or 'spooked' as they read 'danger' into ordinary sights and sounds.

How to help children following such an event

Children need to know that whatever happens, they are loved, they are special and they are not alone.

Children need to feel that they are allowed to express strong feelings of sadness and anger. This may be the first time a child or young person has experienced grief and it can be alarming for both parent and child. Let children know how painful it can be when someone you love dies, and that this pain is a natural part of grieving. It is all right to cry with them and share that pain too.

Parents and other carers need to be aware that an unusually argumentative, irritable and tearful child needs a greater level of understanding.

Children's confidence takes a blow and there may be a fear of separation. Children need a parent or other adult carer to be there to help them regain that confidence. Where practicable, parents and carers may wish to walk to school with children, or to make arrangements for them to walk with friends or join a school run.

However children also enjoy being independent. Once things are more settled, they should be encouraged to do things on their own again.

Even small changes can provide reassurance for a child. It is usual that a child will have to find the way to the bathroom during the night. A low voltage electric light plugged into a socket on the landing makes it a less hazardous adventure. Total darkness may make a child feel disorientated and fearful.

> 'Think', said the minister in Soham, 'of a candle in a dark hall. However feeble its light, however vast the gloom, one flame dispels the darkness.'

If a child is having difficulty settling down to sleep, even after the bedtime story has been read, the warm drink and the hot-water bottle provided, a good idea is to have a radio or a tape or CD playing music or a story quietly by the bedside. Gentle music is soothing and helps a child to relax and changes the tempo of the day.

Physical comforts such as extra clothes when children are feeling out of sorts, can help them to feel snug and warm and protected in a way, like a hug.

Some children lose their appetite, while others 'comfort eat', e.g. crisps for lunch, crisps in between meals. Parents should try to give their children the foods they enjoy; most of us feel overwhelmed when vast quantities of food are placed on a plate in front of us. Small helpings imaginatively arranged on a plate are more tempting. Helping mum or dad to prepare food in the kitchen is companionable and often presents opportunities to talk together over the cake mix. A sense of achievement at having chopped or measured or stirred makes a shepherd's pie look and taste different.

Remembering the dead: school assemblies and services

In one fairly large infant school in 1999 four parents or other close relatives had died during the year. At the annual Christmas service it was decided that the name of each of those who had died would be read out during prayers.

It was a salutary experience to see one small boy sitting in the front row beaming all over his face.

He was so glad that his dad's name had been mentioned.

Though we sometimes react in different ways it does seem that recognition of loss is essential. Adults are often uncertain about the emotional forces they fear they may be unleashing but the acknowledgement of loss is an inevitable part of the healing process.

Of course in a large school community, some people will have had no contact at all with the person who has died; the network of relationships is usually complex. The student may have been a relative stranger to some in their own year group while playing music regularly with students three years older. Nor must we forget the feelings of staff members who taught them.

Despite the fact that it does not seem appropriate to declaim faith and spirituality to a group of students of mixed faith or none, prayer is an essential part of the process. It does not need to be long-winded or to educate. It does need, however, to be present, playing its own part in the context of individual hopes, fears and longings. For even if the particular death is not significant to some school members, it may well bring out feelings associated with other deaths and losses that are very important and, as yet, not fully resolved.

Schools may wish to hold special assemblies after a tragic event to allow pupils an opportunity to reflect and to express their feelings. (For two model assemblies, on 11 September and 'When a child is killed', see the resources available on the National Society's web site. Go to www.natsoc.org.uk/index_fsn.html, then go to 'Autumn term 2002'.)

School memorials

Dependent on age, students who were close to someone who has died long to be able to express (or have expressed on their behalf) their thoughts and feelings.

It is not unusual to find that a few are able to create prose and poetry of considerable quality in response to such events. In moments of powerlessness we value making our contribution however transitory or seemingly inconsequential.

Fashions change, and yet it seems that a thread runs through. Children need something solid to remind them of the person they miss. And so a quiet area, simply planted with a single tree, or with shrubs and a seat, becomes both a place of remembrance and a future resource. Or an illuminated poem, prayer or piece of prose finds pride of place in the school entrance. Whatever is done, try to listen to the views of those most affected before decisions are made.

When the children went back to school in Soham they were asked to gather in the playground as a conclusion to assembly. The headmaster and the vicar had arranged a short symbolic ceremony. Two white doves were set free to fly into the sky. Due to bad weather, they circled not once but three times in order to find their bearings and fly home. A never-to-be-forgotten memory for the children and a cathartic moment for all.

10 After the death: the funeral and beyond

> 'The night before the funeral we all went to the funeral parlour; I'm glad I had a last look at her. I drew a picture for her and wrote a little note on it asking her to wait in heaven for all of us.'

If the family see it as right, the children's sharing of the funeral will happen quite naturally. It is when there are differences of opinion and of culture that this becomes a problem. Nevertheless it is important that children be included in the funeral or memorial service. It is their right. Even young children understand beginnings and endings. We run the risk of forgetting that they too must experience the fact of death, otherwise they are left with an unresolved void. It can even be similar to the emotions experienced by someone whose friend or relative has drowned at sea.

Funeral rites give young and old alike the opportunity to recognize that a change has taken place, and to see that other people loved the dead person and are sad in just the same way as they are. To feel part of a grieving community relieves their sense of 'aloneness'. It enables them to regain some of the confidence lost when they felt in some way that the death was their fault. Being shut out can be far more damaging than facing a new and possibly difficult experience with loving support. Years later a child can look back and be glad that they were included in an important family occasion.

It is helpful if an understanding minister or friend can take the family through the service, explaining what will happen in the church or crematorium. If possible the children should be shown where the grave will be (if there is to be one). Hymns and readings can be chosen together, and perhaps some well-loved music. Reassuring children that a close member of the family or a special friend will sit with them during the service and be there for them afterwards is not only thoughtful – it alleviates the dread of being left alone and not knowing what to do.

> 'The Vicar waffled on about Dad going to heaven, which didn't make up for anything.'

A heartbroken family needs the comfort of knowing that the life of their dead mother or father is cherished and will be long remembered.

The get-together afterwards, though important for getting life back into perspective, can be painful for a child faced with a lot of people talking, all with their own special memories. It brings about a fresh awareness of the person who is no longer there.

Sharon, aged thirteen, writes:

> 'I feel I have the memories I have and other people have no right to tell me they have any more. I don't know what to say to them. My own memories are very special.'

Bereavement brings a crushing sense of isolation. If a family belongs to a local church it is to be hoped they will find strength and comfort in the warmth and friendship there. Continuing pastoral care and a sense of belonging go a long way to ease the tension, and death being part of life can begin to make sense.

If you are the one to whom a bereaved child has turned for help, that child is placing its trust in you. The strong relationship that will be built up between you over a period of time is to be treasured; it will always be part of you, and special. Make sure the child knows where to get in touch with you at any time in the future – just in case, for whatever reason, your reassurance is needed.

11 'Where is God?'

Meanwhile for the bereaved child and for the family who are believers, 'Where is God?'

The question doesn't arise for those who do not believe: for them, with quiet dignity and courage death is simply the end. Not a gateway to eternity, but the end – or perhaps a kind of gateway into a new understanding – that there is nothing wasted in this life, everything depends on everything else, and death is part of a greater and more beautiful pattern.

The believer though, has to come to terms with two things. God is love and if God is in control why do terrible things happen? And secondly, is there a life with God beyond death which somehow makes all the pain bearable?

Christians believe in a God of love, and it is this which is the bedrock of their faith. They see the love of God expressed in the infinite variety and beauty of creation, in the stunning expanses of space, but above all they see the love of God expressed in and through Jesus of Nazareth. As a child put it: 'Jesus put a face on God.' But the kind of love found in Jesus is not sentimental or nostalgic; it is robust, sensitive, open to grief ('Jesus wept'), open to questioning ('Let this cup pass from me') and open to ultimate desolation ('My God, my God, why hast thou forsaken me?').

It is also the kind of love which death cannot conquer, because at the heart of it is the pulsing life of God himself. Jesus, in Christian terms, did not rise from the dead because he was a good man; he rose because God's power could not be held by death.

The resurrection of Jesus is the key. If it happened, then it has the status of a cosmic fact. It is not something that can be undone by not believing. In a sense, whether one believes or not is neither here nor there. If the resurrection is a fact, in the same way that 1066 is a fact, then it is the most astonishing event the universe has witnessed. Christians should not speak about it too glibly. If it is a fact, and if it really happened, then the rest of our lives need to be seen in that light. We don't judge the resurrection by our criteria, it judges us.

It can't be emphasized enough that the resurrection was not a magic trick. Jesus really did die; the heart had stopped; he was, as it were, brain-dead. The Christian belief is that in ways almost impossible to explain, God was in Jesus experiencing the world as a human being, including pain and the absurdity of death. And it is this sense of solidarity between God and his creation which is the ground of our hope.

All of this refers to an event that took place almost two thousand years ago. It was an event with particularity: at a particular time, in a particular place. So what difference can one man's death all those years ago make to our understanding of our deaths now?

The answer would seem to lie in the nature of hope. It is the Christian hope, grounded in the reality of Jesus' death and resurrection, that while that event was particular it also revealed the general and absolute truth of God. It is the nature of God, at all times and in all places, to be a God of love and resurrection.

How then can this affect our understanding now? It is by seeing that there is nothing which lies beyond the grasp of God. Death, the fact, has been broken by resurrection, the fact. Or put another way: the healing love of God can take the degradation and nothingness of death and out of it bring resurgent new life. St Paul put it with eloquent nobility when he wrote:

> 'For I am convinced that there is nothing in death or life, in the realm of spirits or superhuman powers, in the world as it is or the world as it shall be, in the forces of the universe, in heights or depths – nothing in all creation that can separate us from the love of God in Christ Jesus our Lord.' (Romans 8.38-9)

That is the Christian hope expressed in a few profound and powerful words. All of this may be theologically orthodox – tried and tested by Christian minds over the centuries and found to be true – but it doesn't stop the question, 'Why?'. Why does a God of love allow terrible things to happen? It's all very well talking of the redemptive love of God healing even in death, but why does the world have to be so painful in the first place?

There are some answers: none of which are absolutely adequate. One approach talks about the nature of chance in creation. The argument goes like this. If freedom is a necessary part of the creative process – and it would seem to be (look at the way an artist works, it is not robotic) – then freedom has to imply a role for chance. A completely stable universe would be a completely sterile one in which no new things could ever emerge. Newness, or at least the potential for newness, requires an element of chance. If cells can multiply in such a way that new life forms can emerge, then built in to the very fabric of things is the chance that the multiplication of cells could go haywire. Chance is woven into a dance with freedom and newness – and only out of such a dance can self-consciousness and love emerge.

One of the consequences of this approach in relation to God is that it leaves God wrestling with his creation, interacting with it. It does not see him as a divine clock-maker who, having created the machinery, watches it with inscrutable pleasure from a distance. Instead it sees God as intimately involved with the day-to-day unfolding of the universe and therefore intimately involved in every part of our experience. Not outside it, but inside it with us.

There are other Christian doctrines, about the 'Fall' for instance, in which the world is seen as being subject to forces which are 'not-God', which attempt to explain the origins of pain and death in terms of 'sin'. In a nutshell this doctrine says that the world was made perfect, human beings disobeyed God and rebelled against him, and thus sin entered the fabric of things. This doctrine is given powerful metaphorical expression in the stories of Genesis 1 and 2. Jesus' death and resurrection are then seen as the climactic moment in the drama when the forces of darkness are defeated by the self-sacrificial love of Christ.

Perhaps both of these doctrines are necessary for us to understand or to try to come to terms with death. In the end the Christian has to resort to the word 'mystery' to try to explain the relationship between God and his creation. It can be seen as a cop out, to talk of mystery, but perhaps if a mystery is seen not as something to be understood but as something into which we enter, then it is closer to our human experience. It is certainly closer to the life of Jesus of Nazareth; he did not just face death, he went into it. He did not just come alive again, he entered into the resurrection of God.

So, in terms of death and bereavement, where is God? The answer given by Christians is that God does not will sickness; but when sickness and death occur he is in the middle of them helping us to bear our sorrows, sharing the grief, entering into the very depths of our darkness and gently, like a midwife, easing us into new life. And more than that, because of his generous and self-sacrificial love, he takes us through the gateway of Jesus' death and resurrection further on – into eternal life.

Appendix A

Prayers and readings

From *Watership Down*

One chilly, blustery morning in March, I cannot tell exactly how many springs later, Hazel was dozing and waking in his burrow. He had spent a good deal of time there lately, for he felt the cold and could not seem to smell or run so well as in days gone by. He had been dreaming in a confused way – something about rain and elder bloom – when he woke to realise that there was a rabbit lying quietly beside him – no doubt some young buck who had come to ask his advice. The sentry in the run outside should not really have let him in without asking first. Never mind, thought Hazel. He raised his head and said, 'Do you want to talk to me?'

'Yes, that's what I've come for,' replied the other. 'You know me, don't you?'

'Yes of course,' said Hazel, hoping he would be able to remember his name in a moment. Then he saw that in the darkness of the burrow, the stranger's ears were shining with a faint, silver light. 'Yes, my Lord,' he said. 'Yes, I know you.'

'You've been feeling tired,' said the stranger, 'but I can do something about that. I've come to ask you whether you'd care to join my Owsla. We shall be glad to have you and you'll enjoy it. If you're ready, we might go along now.'

They went out past the young sentry, who paid the visitor no attention. The sun was shining and in spite of the cold there were a few bucks and does at play, keeping out of the wind as they nibbled the shoots of spring grass. It seemed to Hazel that he would not be needing his body any more, so he leftit lying on the edge of the ditch, but stopped for a moment to watch his rabbits and to try to get used to the extraordinary feeling that strength and speed were flowing inexhaustibly out of him into their sleek young bodies and healthy senses.

'You needn't worry about them,' said his companion. 'They'll be all right – and thousands like them. If you'll come along, I'll show you what I mean.'

He reached the top of the bank in a single, powerful leap. Hazel followed and together they slipped away, running easily down through the wood, where the first primroses were beginning to bloom.

Richard Adams

Death is nothing at all

Death is nothing at all… I have only slipped away into the next room. I am I, and you are you. Whatever we were to each other, that we are still. Call me by my old familiar name. Speak to me in the easy way which you always used. Put no differences into your tone. Wear no forced air of solemnity or sorrow. Laugh as we always laughed at the little jokes we enjoyed together. Play, smile, think of me. Let my name be ever the household name that it always was. Let it be spoken without effort, without the ghost of a shadow on it. Life means all that it ever meant. It is the same as it ever was. There is absolutely unbroken continuity. What is this death but a negligible accident? Why should I be out of mind because I am out of sight? I am waiting for you for an interval somewhere very near…just round the corner. All is well.

Henry Scott Holland

The gate of the year

I said to the man who stood at the gate of the year, 'Give me a light that I may tread safely into the unknown.' And he replied, 'Go out into the darkness and put your hand into the hand of God. That shall be to you better than light and safer than a known way.'

Minnie Hoskyns

Be thou a bright flame before me,

Be thou a guiding star above me,

Be thou a smooth path below me,

Be thou a kindly shepherd behind me,

Today, tonight, and for ever.

St Columba of Iona

Dear Lord

I would just like to say what a changing place the world is starting to be.

Ever since the Dunblane incident, for example, I, and many others, have become worried and shaky about lots of things.

Whenever I'm on my own, I feel insecure, and if a parent or guardian isn't there to pick me up when I've finished an activity I start to worry.

I would just love it if there was nothing to worry about in the world.

So please, God, help me and everyone else to stay confident and not to worry: through Jesus' name. Amen.

Matthew Neville (age 11)

I had thought that your death

was a waste and a destruction,

a pain of grief hardly to be endured.

I am only beginning to learn

that your life was a gift and a growing

and a loving left with me.

The desperation of death

destroyed the existence of love,

but the fact of death

cannot destroy what has been given.

I am learning to look at your life again

instead of your death and your departing.

Marjorie Pizer

Lord in heaven,

you have promised us new life

through your Son, Jesus.

Help us to live with that promise

in our hearts and in our lives,

so that our sadness can be turned by you

into strength and blessing for the days ahead.

Christopher Herbert

Lord, make me an instrument of your peace.

Where there is hatred, let me sow love,

Where there is injury, pardon,

Where there is doubt, faith,

Where there is despair, hope,

Where there is darkness, light,

Where there is sadness, joy.

Grant that I may not so much seek to be consoled as
to console,

Not so much to be understood as to understand,

Not so much to be loved, as to love;

For it is in giving that we receive,

It is in pardoning that we are pardoned, it is in dying that we
awake to eternal life.

Attributed to Francis of Assisi

God in heaven

give us understanding

give us strength

give us peace

today, tomorrow and for evermore.

No matter what happens dear God

we know that your light is stronger than any darkness

and that you are always with us,

now and for ever and ever.

Christopher Herbert

Lord, all these years we were so close to one another, we did everything together, we seemed to know what each other was feeling, without the need of words, and now she is gone. Every memory hurts . . . sometimes there comes a feeling that she is near, just out of sight. Sometimes I feel your reproach that to be so submerged in grief is not to notice that she is as eager to keep in touch with me, as I with her. O dear Lord, I pray out of a sore heart that it may be so, daring to believe that it can be so.

George Appleton

Lord, we look up to you
and receive from you
your blessing
your strength
your most holy love.
In the darkest moments of our lives,
O God let us remember that you are the light
you are the hope
you are the courage we need.

Christopher Herbert

Into that house they shall enter
and in that house they shall dwell
where there shall be
  no cloud nor sun
  no darkness nor dazzling
but one equal light;
  no noise nor silence
but one equal music;
  no fears nor hopes
but one equal possession;
  no foes nor friends
but one equal eternity.

Keep us, Lord,
so awake in the duties of our callings
that we may thus sleep in peace
and wake in thy glory.

John Donne

Eternal Lord God, grant me a glimpse into the new order of being into which your child has now entered; may he feel at home there and continue to grow in happiness, holiness, maturity and love. I thank you that our relationships of love cannot be broken by physical death. I cannot but be sad that he is out of physical sight, yet not out of touch, for we are both in your hands and nothing harmful can hurt us. Unto your gracious mercy and protection we commit him. May he see the smile of your welcome and smile back in warm gratitude and love, O Father of souls.

George Appleton

We shall rest and we shall see, we shall see and we shall love, we shall love and we shall praise, in the end which is no end.

St Augustine

For I am convinced that neither death, nor life, nor angels, nor rulers, nor height, nor depth, nor anything else in all creation, will be able to separate us from the love of God in Christ Jesus our Lord.

Romans 8.38-9

For God so loved the world that he gave his only Son, so that everyone who believes in him may not perish but have eternal life.

John 3.16

For the Lamb at the centre of the throne will be their shepherd, and he will guide them to springs of the water of life, and God will wipe away every tear from their eyes.

Revelation 7.17

O Father of all, we pray to thee for those whom we love, but see no longer. Grant them thy peace; let light perpetual shine upon them; and in thy loving wisdom and almighty power work in them the good purpose of thy perfect will; through Jesus Christ our Lord. Amen.

The Prayer Book as Proposed in 1928

Merciful Father,

hear our prayers and comfort us;

renew our trust in your Son,

whom you raised from the dead;

strengthen our faith

that [*N* and] all who have died in the love of Christ

will share in his resurrection;

who lives and reigns with you,

now and for ever.

Amen.

Common Worship: Pastoral Services, p. 350

Lord God,
you are attentive to the voice of our pleading.
Let us find in your Son
comfort in our sadness,
certainty in our doubt
and courage to live.
Make our faith strong
through Christ our Lord.
Amen.

Common Worship: Pastoral Services, p. 357

N, go forth from this world:
in the love of God the Father who created you,
in the mercy of Jesus Christ who redeemed you,
in the power of the Holy Spirit who strengthens you.
May the heavenly host sustain you
and the company of heaven enfold you.
In communion with all the faithful,
may you dwell this day in peace.
Amen.

Common Worship: Pastoral Services, p. 376

Appendix B

To whom do we turn?

Local sources of help

General practitioner

School doctor

Educational psychologist

Local paediatrician

Paediatric community nurses

Hospice/hospital and attached social worker

Macmillan nurse (through Health Authority)

Clergy and pastoral assistants

Social worker – through Social Services

Educational Welfare Officer

Citizens Advice Bureau (can give advice and information on everything including counselling services)

Samaritans

Colleagues

Friends who know the child well

Your own friends, for moral support

CRUSE

Cruse House, 126 Sheen Road, Richmond, Surrey, TW9 1UR

Tel: 020 8940 4818

www.crusebereavementcare.org.uk

The national organization for the bereaved and their children.

National Association of Widows

1st Floor, Neville House, 14 Waterloo Street, Birmingham, B2 5TX

Tel: 024 7663 4848

ACT

Institute of Child Health, Royal Hospital for Sick Children, St Michael's Hill, Bristol, BS2 8BJ

Tel: 0117 927 6998

Action for the care of families whose children have life-threatening and terminal conditions.

Compassionate Friends

53 North Street, Bristol, BS3 1EN

Tel: 0117 953 9639

www.compassionatefriends.org

Bereaved parents offer friendship and understanding to other bereaved parents.

Parents of Murdered Children Support Group

10 Eastern Avenue, Pridwell, Southend on Sea, Essex, SS2 5QU

Tel: 01702 68510

Part of Compassionate Friends.

Twins and Multiple Births Association (TAMBA)

TAMBA, PO Box 30, Little Sutton, South Wirral, L66 1TH

Tel: 0870 770 3305

www.tamba.org.uk

Includes a bereavement support group.

SANDS

28 Portland Place, London, W1N 4DE

Tel: 020 7436 7940

www.uk-sands.org

Stillbirth and neonatal deaths.

St Christopher's Hospice Information Service

51–59 Lawrie Park Road, Sydenham, London, SE26 6DZ

Tel: 020 8778 9252

Information about hospices nationwide plus mail order bookshop and library service.

The Child Bereavement Trust
Aston House, High Street, West Wycombe, Buckinghamshire, HP14 3AG.

Information and Support Line:
Tel: 0845 357 1000

www.childbereavement.org.uk

Information, support and training for professionals caring for bereaved families.

Sudden Death Support Association
Dolphin Lane, Swallowfield, Reading, Berkshire, RG7 1TB

Tel: 01189 889797

An organization to help relatives and close friends of people who die suddenly.

CARE confidential
Freephone: 0800 0282228

For pregnancy and post-abortion concerns.

SeeSaw
Bush House, 2 Merewood Avenue, Oxford, OX3 8EF

Tel: 01865 744768

Bereavement support for children in Oxfordshire. Training programme for professionals.

MEDITEC specialist book service
Swan House, 44 High Street, Walton on Thames, Surrey, KT12 1BY

Tel: 01932 244899

Supplier of medical books and reference texts.

The Child Death Helpline
Freephone: 0800 282986

A freephone service for all those affected by the death of a child.

The Candle Project at St Christopher's Hospice
51–59 Lawrie Park Road, Sydenham, London, SE26 6DZ

Tel: 0208 778 9252

Bereavement help for children, young people and families.

SAMM (Support after Murder and Manslaughter)
Tel: 020 8657 9194

The Way Foundation
Tel: 0870 011 3450

www.wayfoundation.org.uk

Providing a way forward for the widowed and young.

Appendix C

Books and resources

Children up to 7 years

Badger's Parting Gifts

Susan Varley

(Harper Collins, ISBN 0 006 62398 0)

Badger is quite unafraid of dying. His only worry was how his friends would feel when he was gone. When they find his goodbye note they are sad but come to realize that he has left each one of them a parting gift. A picture book for explaining death to children.

Waterbugs and Dragonflies: explaining death to children

Doris Stickney and Gloria Ortiz

(Mowbray, ISBN 0 264 66904 5)

An analogy for human life on earth and life after death: the waterbug's life under water, and its emergence into the world above the water as a dragonfly.

I'll Always Love You

Hans Wilhelm

(Hodder & Stoughton, ISBN 0 340 40153 2)

The story of the love between and boy and his dog who dies. A reassuring and gentle book for a child who has recently suffered the death of a pet.

Children 7–12 years

A Bridge to Terabithia

Katherine Peterson

(Puffin, ISBN 0 140 36628 0)

In their make-believe world of Terabithia, Leslie and Jess are invincible. So when something terrible happens, Jess finds he can face grief and disaster better than he could ever have imagined.

Red Sky in the Morning

E. Laird

(Macmillan, ISBN 0 330 30890 4)

Anna's baby brother is born with spina bifida and dies months later. The book contains much humour but it also illustrates the emotional difficulties that children can face when they have a sibling with a physical disability.

Remembering Grandad

Sheila Isherwood and Kate Isherwood

(Oxford University Press, ISBN 0 192 72368 5)

Remembering a much-loved grandfather.

Someone Who Died Suddenly

Available from St Christopher's Hospice Bookshop

51–59 Lawrie Park Road, Sydenham, London, SE26 6DZ

Tel: 020 8768 4660

This booklet guides children through the aftermath of an unexpected death, and includes information on procedures such as inquests and funerals.

Someone Special has Died

Available from St Christopher's Hospice Bookshop

A bestseller at St Christopher's. Aimed at children up to 11 years, adults also have found it useful. It describes emotions likely to be felt after bereavement and describes what happens to a body after death.

Children 11+

Vicky Angel

Jacqueline Wilson

(Doubleday, ISBN 0 385 60040 2)

Jade is so used to being with and agreeing with Vicky, her larger-than-life best friend, that when a tragic accident occurs, she can hardly believe that Vicky's no longer there. Amusing and entertaining story of Jade's struggle with her own feelings, the reactions of her family and friends and her final acceptance of life without Vicky.

Your Friend Rebecca

Linda Hoy

(Harper Collins, ISBN 0 003 3001 7)

Rebecca and her father mourn the loss of a mother and wife, each with their own grief and unable to respond to that of the other. At school through drama and the reading of King Lear, Rebecca begins to understand herself and gradually begins to communicate with her father, until eventually they are able to share their pain.

Straight Talk about Death for Teenagers

E. Grollman

(Econo-Clad Books, ISBN 0 7857 1987 3)

Explains to teenagers what to expect when someone they love dies. The book discusses normal reactions to the shock of death, how grief can affect personal relationships and other topics to help work through it.

River Boy

T. Bowler

(Oxford University Press, ISBN 0 192 75158 1)

Poetic and surreal images of water and swimming are used to deal with the difficult subjects of death and loss in an accessible and affecting way.

Your Parent has Died

Available from St Christopher's Hospice Bookshop

This booklet is for young teenagers whose parent has died. It highlights a few thoughts common to young people at this time and comments on them – e.g. 'things I didn't say'; 'I just want to talk'; 'is it OK to forget about it sometimes?'

Books for adults

The Lone Twin: understanding Twin Bereavement and Loss

J. Woodward

(Free Association Books, ISBN 1 8534 3374 8)

The loss of a twin can be devastating for the survivor. Joan Woodward includes parental attitudes to the surviving twin, the surviving twin's guilt, the ability to cope and the effect of loss in childhood and in adulthood. Of particular interest, perhaps, to those who lost their twin at birth.

A Special Scar: the experiences of people bereaved by suicide

Alison Wertheimer

(Routledge, ISBN 0 425 22027 0)

A valuable book which looks in detail at the stigma surrounding suicide and offers practical help for survivors, relations and friends of people who have taken their own life.

Through Grief

Elizabeth Collick

(Darton, Longman & Todd, ISBN 0 232 51682 0)

Published in association with CRUSE.

This book is intended to help us understand the confused feelings of bereavement, so that we can in turn help our children. It will be of help not only to the bereaved themselves, but also to doctors, nurses, clergy, social workers and relations and friends of someone coping with bereavement.

Helping children cope with separation and loss

Claudia Jewett

(Batsford, ISBN 0 7134 7766 0)

Published in association with British Agencies for Adoption and Fostering.

A study of children and adolescents facing the stress of all kinds of loss. A practical down-to-earth book with examples of children losing parents through death or divorce or through disruptive foster placements.

Am I Allowed to Cry? A study of bereavement among people who have learning difficulties

Maureen Oswin

(Souvenir Press, ISBN 0 2856 5096 3)

An important book that draws attention to the special problems of being bereaved among people with learning difficulties.

All in the End is Harvest: an anthology for those who grieve

Agnes Whitaker

(Dartman, Longman & Todd, ISBN 0 232 51624 3)

Published in association with CRUSE.

An inspired selection of extracts of prose and poetry known to have been of real help to bereaved people.

Helping Children Cope with Grief: facing a death in the family

Rosemary Wells

(Sheldon Press, ISBN 0 859 6955 9)

A book for parents, friends, teachers, clergy, doctors and nurses – anyone who is trying to help a child to come to terms with death. For the problems special to terminal illness or sudden death, or the death of a family member in an unhappy home.

Prayers for Children

Compiled by Christopher Herbert

(National Society/Church House Publishing, ISBN 0 7151 4816 8)

A rich and imaginative resource book which will inspire parents, teachers, clergy and everyone involved in nurturing children's faith.

Death in the Classroom

Eleanor D. Gatliffe

(Epworth Press, ISBN 0 7162 0441 X)

A resource book for adults who help children and young people come to terms with death.

Words of Comfort

Christopher Herbert

(National Society/Church House Publishing, second edition, 2000, ISBN 0 7151 4941 5)

A book to bring comfort to the bereaved: sensitive and full of faith, but unafraid to face the darkness.

It includes prayers and writings both old and new, reflecting the pain and joy of the journey through bereavement.